To: Tammy –

Every minute, every hour of every day,
brings the opportunity of wonderful gifts of
joy in life. But, the greatest of all –
is in finding a new friend.
I hope that you will enjoy the expressions
of life in the pages following.

    Affectionately inscribed,
      Your friend –

      Richard Sweeting

October 30, 2012

RIVERS
of TIME

A COLLECTION
OF SELECTED
POETIC WORKS

RICHARD G.
MORIARTY

WestBow Press books may be ordered through booksellers or by contacting:

WestBow Press
A Division of Thomas Nelson
1663 Liberty Drive
Bloomington, IN 47403
www.westbowpress.com
1-(866) 928-1240

ISBN: 978-1-4497-6457-9 (e)
ISBN 978-1-4497-6458-6 (sc)

Library of Congress Control Number: 2012915764

Printed in the United States of America

WestBow Press rev. date: 09/12/2012

WestBow
PRESS
A DIVISION OF THOMAS NELSON

CONTENTS

Dedication

To my wife, Janet,
who encouraged me to compile these writings
and raised me up when I became discouraged.

To my children,
Mary Catherine, Richard, and Cullen,
who through the years have brought me so much
joy, pride, and love.

Together with
my extended-family children,
Jennifer,
who urged me to write and to continue to do so
even when I had doubts about myself,
Travis and Shanti,
who have brought such caring and love into our family,
and my grandchildren,
Shelbie, Lydia, Samuel, Isaac, and Judah —
all the love of my life.

Introduction

When writing poetry, I write literally for myself.

Poetic writing comes in many forms, styles, and types. My personality dictates
my own style. I do not vary very much from the way I am. One's expression
is an extension of one's self, and that is what you are about to read.

I am a restless person, usually one who will multitask when doing things.
I jump around a lot. That is why two of the poems in this collection,
"I Am Who I Am" and "Searching," describe a lot about me.

There are many folks in this life who are similar to me in style and habit. I feel sorry
for you, but we are who we are, and for that reason alone must go on through this
life in search of those things that continually elude us. That is what makes this life
so terribly interesting, frustrating, and, at the same time, fun and challenging.

The writings assembled in this collection are mine and represent
my views and feelings on a number of subject areas.

I hope that you will enjoy reading them as much as I enjoyed writing them.

— Richard G. Moriarty

Man in the Arena

"It is not the critic who counts; not the man who points out how the strong man stumbles, or where the doer of deeds could have done them better. The credit belongs to the man who is actually in the arena, whose face is marred by dust and sweat and blood, who strives valiantly; who errs and comes short again and again; because there is not effort without error and shortcomings; but who does actually strive to do the deed; who knows the great enthusiasm, the great devotion, who spends himself in a worthy cause, who at the best knows in the end the triumph of high achievement and who at the worst, if he fails, at least he fails while daring greatly. So that his place shall never be with those cold and timid souls who know neither victory nor defeat."

— Theodore Roosevelt, "Citizenship in a Republic,"
speech at the Sorbonne, Paris, April 23, 1910

Section I
RIVERS OF TIME

Rivers of Time

꧁❖꧂

Like rivers of time, our lives drift by
as seasons, providing for the trees,
which acquire soft, green leaves, and then in time,
turning red and golden, shed their leaves.

Travelers in time are all like a wind,
sweeping across the plains of life — visitors in a temporary land —
enjoying moments of bright, sunny days filled with fun and joy,
soon to be followed by sudden storms
and then dark hours, followed again by
the brightness of the day; rivers of time,
carrying each traveler through the day, waiting,
waiting for the next to arrive.

Time, an ever-moving thing, a river,
carrying each person in turbulent white water
or calm, flowing streams through all events of life,
then stranding one on a rocky and barren shore or
gently laying one upon soft and lush meadows
to rest, as in a quiet and calm place.

Finally, on the appointed day, a call goes forth, and
the wayfarer receives a summons to go quickly,
moving through time to stand in a queue, moving to an unknown space
together with others summoned to appear at some distant place.

The queue is formed, and the line moves forward; the time has arrived
to board those great ships of time, like the giant Leviathan casts
off from near harbors and then ever moving
to arrive at some distant shore.

Like rivers of time, our lives drift by a season at a time,
travelers all, in a moment in time.

Straw Men and Problems

His hair was yellow, pieces of straw
sticking out the sides every which way,
standing tall and mute, not a word, just looking cute.
Life's problems not being faced,
left to their own, unattended, drifting,
like a straw cast in the wind.
Wonder why this is considered a sin?
Heartaches and worries all about, you see,
but no one to solve them but you and me.
That's all around us. Do we see
straw men and problems
left for you and me?
Things get solved by doing and sometimes failing,
not by standing tall, mute, and cute.
Mistakes are made,
lessons are learned,
trial and error.
Sometimes we get burned.
That's how to face the world that we see,
not being a straw man, but working together — just you and me.

Dreams

I dream of beautiful things,
things that I love to see and feel.

I dream of waterfalls
and see the sparkle of sunlight through the water
that from its radiant color forms a rainbow
and hear the rush of wind as it falls far below.

I think of a flower
and dream of the perfect nature of a petal,
the sprinkling of color so perfectly settled,
uplifting in its nature.

I see birds soaring in the sky
and dream of their soft call as they seek
another from far away.

I dream of one who loves me
as deeply as I love her
and dream of her touch on my bare skin
and feel the warm caress of parted lips.

I dream of a baby sleeping quietly in a bed
and see the faint smile
as the infant dreams likewise of butterflies
skipping across cloudless skies.

I think of children and dream
of them running across a field
and hear them arguing over who
was the fastest of them all.

It's been written that we can dream
but we should not let dreams become our masters.
I am enslaved to my dreams;
shameless and unafraid,
I dream and bow
to my master.

Old Shoes

I opened the closet and walked on in;
my foot hit something that had fallen from its bin.
An old pair of shoes, wrinkled and worn,
lay out on the floor, reminding me of a long lost friend.

Quite a story old shoes can tell,
where we've gone, a life that's been lived well.
Oh, I know that some folks
don't care about the past,
only the present, because times are just too fast.

But old shoes go slow,
with memories from so long ago
of times good and bad,
smiles and tears,
of things happy and sad.

Old shoes are like friends; they stay around
in good times and bad.
They are really quite sound.

At times, we struggle in life to find
a place of happiness, peace, and a companion to be kind.
Old shoes are with us every step of the way,
through good times and bad,
bright days and sad.

Old shoes are like good friends
you don't throw away.
Just tuck them back
and bring them out another day.

Faraway Friend

Fragrant flower,
faraway friend.
Heaven's scent.

Once in Time

A road that goes and doesn't come back,
a train that travels a one-way track.
Life seems long and hard sometimes,
but then a new day breaks
and all seems fine,
for we travel this way but once in time.

Now and again we need our friends,
some folks to lean on when times are tough,
people who are made of real strong stuff,
those to guide us and point the way
when we get lost and don't know what to say,
friends who will follow after us
to show us that all can be fine,
for we pass this way just once in time.

It takes a village to raise a child
because life does not always act so mild.
Things are dealt us along the way
that make this life seem not so gay,
but there's no need to get distressed,
for there is a way to deal with this mess.
All we need is to try to be kind,
for we pass this way but once in time.

God has given us strength for the day,
and we all know that He has the final say.
Life is fickle, we are told,
and we should face our problems and try to be bold.
Just strive and seek and hope to find,
for we pass this way but once in time.

Blaze of Glory

A sudden scurry of light
flashed across the darkened sky.
Cosmic particles flew across
the horizon, creating enough light to
attract these wandering eyes.
A fiery display like fireflies
leaving a trail of glowing embers,
weaving a pattern of radiant light
through the darkened night.
A sense of cosmic games being played
by bodies as old as time itself,
falling from heaven's grace
in a flood of color and flames.
Across the sky, comets moving like balloons
on strings delight children
looking into the night.
Again appeared in that expanse of space
the death of a faraway star,
blazing its eerie trail across the night sky,
leaving momentarily a ribbon of light, then to be seen
no more.
A celestial grand plan put in place
by other than man; only He could devise
such a thing — to hang stars as ornaments
in the sky, leaving man to provide only
names for someone else's scheme.

Everything in life has its time and place,
yet what more to seek but not to find
than a falling star to treat these old eyes of mine.

Whenever our call comes to follow these flaming beauties,
shall we go quietly to a darkened space,
or shall we, like these celestial things, leave this life

in a blaze of glory — a lasting moment of beauty and
grace — as we move on to some other place?

Un Lieu de Paix

There is a special place where quiet people go
when times get tense and mean,
a place where life seems much calmer — and truly serene,
a place where gentle spirits can go
with wounded hearts or fearful souls — un lieu de paix, a place of peace,
where sounds and fury all cease.

Far away from noise and prying eyes,
soft sounds and quiet times abound.
Un lieu de paix, a place of peace,
away from all the turbulent sounds.

Days of blue skies, green meadows, and slow-moving streams,
a land of quiet and pleasant dreams.
Purple flowers brighten slow walks along a country road,
red and yellow ones too —
never knew what they were called,
just beautiful color like a rainbow's hue.

High overhead, fluffy clouds float by,
colorful birds soar on high.
A place of peace where children play,
with the sound of small voices laughing
while echoing calls of a dare
as they chase butterflies and dandelion blooms
that drift like small parachutes through the air.

The smell of fresh-baked pies set out to cool
drift through an open window.
An old rocking chair waits on the porch,
a place of rest from the warm day's sun,
comforted by an old dog sleeping nearby,
makes this world a place of quiet — and fun.

Away from all the noise and confusion of the day,
to a special world of escape from the fray,
a place where quiet people go
when times get tense and mean,
a place where life seems much more calm — and truly serene.

A place far away from sounds and prying eyes,
where soft sounds and quiet times abound.
Un lieu de paix, a place of peace,
away from all the turbulent sounds.

Where Have You Gone, Little Boy?

Where have you gone, little boy
with the dark curly hair
and the skinny body?
I used to see you run and play
and chase lightning bugs and baseballs.
Where have you gone, little boy
with the sparkle in your eyes
and the giggle when you chased the butterflies?
Where is the laughter that came with practical jokes
and flowers picked by the side of the road to
surprise your mother as she met you at the door?
That little boy is still close by,
only now he sits in his overstuffed chair
and dozes in the warm spring air,
no longer chasing butterflies and baseballs
but content to watch foolish things on
that idiot box.
Why don't you come out and play, little boy?
Life is not much fun when there is no one to run and play with.

Time

There is a time for everything, we are told,
a time to enjoy, work, and then grow old.

As a season comes and goes,
time moves through our lives as quickly as a wind that blows.

For every day that we are given,
there is a time for things for which must be striven.

For work that must be done,
there is little time for things that are fun.

Time can be a friend indeed,
but only when we seek someone in need.

Our time on earth is to be spent
doing things that are meant.

When our time is finally at an end,
then it will be determined how much we have sinned.

The time in this life that we have spent
will determine where it is we are to be sent.

Morning Mist and Summer Rain

Far away from the noise of the city
I walked in the quiet of a country lane,
nothing to distract me this day,
but the morning mist
turning into a summer rain.

I was born to be free from my troubles,
born to smell the freshness of the day,
nothing to accompany me on my trip,
but the morning mist turning into a summer rain.

There are times when I must be free,
away from the cares and worries of this life,
when I can walk alone in this world
with nothing but the morning mist turning into a summer rain.

Sometimes in all my wanderings
I talk with my God up above.
It's amazing what I will hear,
when walking in a morning mist turning into a summer rain.

A symphony of sounds are present
from the creatures who live nearby,
from the call of a coyote drifting on the wind
to the birds in their nests where they lie.
All add to the beauty of this day
when filled with nothing but a morning
mist turning into a summer rain.

My love for life is all around
given by a God who cares from up above.
It is seen most clearly on a country lane
when walking in a morning mist turning into a summer rain.

Skin Don't Matter, Effort Do

White and black,
Red and brown,
Yellow too.
Colors only.
Makes no difference
what the skin.
It's the result of the effort
that the person makes
that tells the measure of the soul.
Made by God,
one and all,
each a value to Him.
A joy to His sight
is each person,
not the skin.

Solitude

From far out at sea,
the errant wave begins,
pushed onward by a restless tide and wind,
rushing headlong toward the shore
in a mad dash to find a home
on some lonely and distant place.
The sound of the wave
crashing down upon the surf
brings a constant and noisy roar
only to summon another to repeat its chore.
Never-ending tide and wave
crash constantly on the shore
to make a symphony of sound
that lulls a nearby sun worshiper
into a deep and restful sleep.

Lazy Day

The water was
dark and brown.
Two turtles rested on a nearby log,
soaking in the sun.

A large gray heron swooped lazily down,
landing effortlessly
while looking around for a tasty morsel.

Overhead, a squawking jay served as sentinel
to warn of my intrusion into its domain.

All I wanted was to sit and dip a line
into the cool, brown pool.

Perhaps an unsuspecting fish would seek
the dangling worm on the end of my line.

Even if there were no takers,
I wouldn't mind.

It was just a chance to visit
the calm and quiet of that dark and cool
pool as it just drifted by.

Thoughts of nothingness clouded an
otherwise empty mind.

It was just a lazy day,
warm and friendly sitting by that
dark and brown pool
with a drifting line.

Cares drifted away
like the white, fluffy clouds high above.

So why spoil a beautiful day?

Searching

Like a restless wind that blows across our lives,
our souls search through doors only to find boundless sighs.
Always seeking, but not yet finding
answers to questions that never stop hiding.

Many souls are always searching,
following the restless winds of life,
like companions on a journey, all seek to find
unknown answers to questions that have no sign.

Not a stone unturned, not a road not traveled,
always looking as though with a common thread binding
this band of travelers seeking, but not finding.

A restless wind blows across our lives,
like the universe that never ends.
Searching, searching, never growing weary
for the chase of an answer that life won't send.
Not too far, but yet so far, we run about
on a quest for life that has no end.

Quite a band of travelers are we,
who seek to find, but yet cannot see.
Always searching, like a restless wind,
blowing across our lives
on another chase to send.

Who can be satisfied in a world known
when there is so much to seek?
That is like the wind that has blown,
always seeking, but not yet finding
answers to questions that never stop hiding.

*Dedicated to James Kavanaugh, whose There are Men
Too Gentle to Live Among Wolves gave me the inspiration
to write this poem. I, too, am a searcher in life.*

New Day Given

With the setting of the sun
another day has been won.
Deep purple and red skies blend together,
mark the memories of another day forever.

Once, a long, long time ago,
my days seemed so dark and forlorn.
But then I realized that with the passage of each
I had but to listen to the words of a sage,
words that had been handed down through the age,
that from the beauty of the setting sun
came the anticipation of the glorious sunrise of another one.

Time can heal all wounds of pride and heart.
Each day can bring bright rays of joy for a new start.
The beauty of the setting sun
reminds me of another day being won.

How I love to see each day that I'm given,
to know that I have striven
to bring to my heart a joy of a life lived
and the anticipation of the sunrise of a new day given.

I Am Who I Am

A restless soul am I,
never satisfied with what I find,
seeking that which is new to me.
Made by God as I am — I am who I am.

Torn between the rules of life.
Following them causes me much strife.
Bored with the same old humdrum,
always moving on to something new.
Made by God as I am — I am who I am.

Other folks are just like me,
searching for answers on a restless sea,
tossed about like a ship without a rudder.
Made by God as I am — I am who I am.

Recurring tasks becoming boring so soon,
following the same old game is a downer.
Restless by nature, always seeking a new game.
Made by God as I am — I am who I am.

New sunrises are exciting.
New days always bring hope for horizons not seen,
searching for the mysteries of life in a never-ending game.
Made by God as I am — I am who I am.

Life is but a challenge to seek.
Mysteries are but puzzles to solve.
Each day is but a day to enjoy.
Made by God as I am — I am who I am.

Section II
SEASONS OF TIME

Whistle-Stop

It sits empty and sad,
having gone from good to bad.
Where once there were people,
now there is only a vacant steeple.
The church is bare, except for a few.
There's not much left, only the morning dew.
Like so many places across this land,
this old whistle-stop sits closed and broken down.
Where once as children we played, catching fireflies
in Mason jars and dancing with sparklers in the front yard,
now the homes are closed and falling in.
The stores and movie and grocery, too,
stand bare and empty with nothing left to do.
Down the street, there is hardly a trace
of the old school, so that we wouldn't recognize the place.
We called this old whistle-stop home,
and memories we still keep.
Every time the freight passes, it makes us leap.
Fireflies still light the nighttime summer sky,
and millions of stars still live close by.
So even if the train doesn't stop anymore
and all that is left is its mournful whistle,
home it is, and home it will be,
no matter if there is nothing left for us to see.

Music in the Air

The early sounds of the day
begin to be heard even before the sun has risen.
One by one, sounds are added as the great city awakens
like an orchestra warming up
in anticipation of the conductor arriving —
sounds of a garbage truck making its early rounds,
with the clanking of cans and moving of dumpsters,
a bevy of people beginning to move about,
shuffling through the streets,
honking of horns as impatient drivers try
to muscle their way by,
an army of people crowding the sidewalk and
marching off to work, disturbed by the sudden
backfire of a truck
and deafened by the loud rap from the window of a passing car.
All seem to surround us no matter where we are.
It's not the noises of the street that are heard,
but the birth of the music in the air.

No matter how many sounds we hear,
they bring no noise that we need fear.
But rather it is a melody drifting by,
each adding its own distinct sound
and giving us music in the air.

The noises of the street
marry as a symphony of sound,
each adding to the tune that is heard,
an orchestra flowing from all around and
placing music in the air.

The melodies drift softly by,
mingled with the crash of the loudest note,
each adding to the rush of a blended sound,
placing music in the air.

No matter where we turn
or how far that we go,
it's not the noises of the street
that we hear, but
the music in the air.

There Is an Anger in This Land

꧁ ꧂

There is an anger in this land,
one that is not to hard to understand.
It comes from a lack of trust
of those we elected to represent us.

This nation was created as one under God.
It was built by workers of the sod,
people from all walks and faiths of life
Coming to a land free of strife.

From the humble beginnings of an early time,
when a people who came with a yearning to be free,
throwing off the shackles of tyranny,
established a government elected to represent the many.

As time went on, the government grew
until it reached the point where it was run by a few.
Lost in time was the point of view
that the government was designed to keep the people free.

Full circle we are coming in this land that was free
to once more subjected to a form of tyranny.
Now that banner our forebears flew
is again unfurled with its message for all to see:
"Don't tread on me."

The Big Easy

꙳

Brash lady of the South, home of jazz and blues,
party town USA, brawling port of the nation,
melting pot of cultures, the city of hope,
and queen of the Nile of the Americas.

She's the Big Easy.

Yes, I know there is Bourbon Street,
where you rub shoulders with pimps, prostitutes,
drunks, and movie queens,
stand shoulder to shoulder and jostle and fight for the
cheap beads thrown from a Mardi Gras float,
walk the narrow, crowded streets and listen to
the mournful moan of the blues,
the rhythm of jazz being discovered as it drifts
through the narrow alleyways,
feel the sweat and the clamor of the docks,
with the nation's exports being loaded on the
mammoth ships for all the world,
sip the strong coffee and wash down the beignets,
savor the dripping po' boys and famous oysters Rockefeller,
and smell the aromas of the seafood preparer of the nation.

She is the queen city of the Nile of the Americas—
the mighty Missisip'.

Don't apologize for her being
a lady of the streets,
the birthplace of jazz,
the queen city of the mighty river of the nation.
Good food.
Fun time.
Fast people.

She's the city that never sleeps,
the play town and workplace of the nation,
a lady like no other lady.

She's the Big Easy.

Armadillo

❧❦❧

They came in the night,
nocturnal mammals plying their trade,
armored carriers of an age-old scourge,
a modern-day version of a creature from a Mesolithic age,
rooting in the soil for their tasty grubs and morsels,
leaving behind holes in the lawns and uprooted freshly planted beds,
a total destruction of a day's labor in the garden.
Anger arises from the waste and want of the destroyed beauty.
A plan, a trap for these ancient creatures cunningly devised.
Arising in the night,
waiting with gun and light,
ever vigilant for the coming of these armored destroyers.
Waiting, waiting, as the day begins to break,
but not to be seen after a long night through
bleary eyes and exhausted from a sleepless night.
Another day, another night, a new plan to be devised
to see if they come,
seeking the tasty grubs lying beneath freshly planted beauties.
A combat to be waged with these armored creatures of old.
A test of wills to see who will win out.

The Old Man and the Mule

A faint outline appeared in the early morn.
A full moon still shed its light, dark shadows
spread across the land casting an eerie
shadow over the far distant hills.
An old buckboard clattered along a dusty road,
bumping roughly over pot holes
washed out by an early winter rain.

The old mule plodded along,
ribs showing from a life of hard work prolonged,
a rather tired animal trudging slowly along,
tugging at its heavy load.

The old man sat humped over on the seat,
nodding as though he were asleep.
A low-hanging branch served to awaken him as
it slapped sharply against the side of his head,
causing him to sit up straight, grabbing his hat
that was about to be shed.

A road traveled more than once,
from the old farm down to the general store,
bumping along on rutted roads, filled with
holes, not a friendly ride it was, but
one that both the rider and mule
had made many times.

On either side of the road rows of tall trees standing straight
with leaves long since gone, the trunks
appearing as gaunt ribs rising up from the ground
much as the old mule appeared,
as it pulled its heavy load quietly by.

The day was cold; a north wind blew, chilling
both with icy fingers that cut to the bone.
But the old man and the mule just plodded along,
going silently down that dusty road, bumping
over the ruts and pot holes worn by time and use itself.
Two old friends working and waiting, serving out time
as they repeated their daily chores.

Time and work take their toll,
as man and beast move along
worn and traveled roads,
doing never-ending chores of old
until the end of a road is finally reached.

Section III
TROUBLES OF TIME

Street of Broken Dreams

There is a place far from here,
a land full of bitter tears,
a place where lonely folks can go
when they seek to mend broken hearts
and find lost dreams.

A land of winding lonely streets,
dark places where the sad ones come
walking alone with shattered memories,
known only as the street of broken dreams.

It is a land of bitter memories,
dark dreams, and broken hearts,
a place far from here, where only
the lonely can walk
on the streets of broken dreams.

The sun rarely shines on these stained walks.
Dark shadows mar their way.
Sadness and bitter tears are their signposts
on these empty streets of broken dreams.

Those who come may linger awhile,
seeking to find their way,
until at last their journey brings them
to the end of their street of broken dreams.

Closets of our Lives

Dark shadows drift against a wall.
Deep gloom penetrates the prisons of our souls.
Things that live from a darkened past
dominate lives that have surrendered with continually downcast eyes,
keeping us locked in the closets of our lives.

Locked in a perpetual state of the past,
prisoners of tear-stained days
and continuing nights of gloom,
not allowing a light to break into our hidden rooms,
lost souls surrendered to a darkened past,
keeping us locked in the closets of our lives.

Walking through the shadows of today.
Memories of a heartache of yesterday
weigh heavily on us each passing day,
keeping us locked in the closets of our lives.

Living with the trials of our lives,
bitter tears streaming down pale cheeks.
Not able to walk in the light of day,
keeping us chained to the wall
of the closets of our lives.

Clenched fists pound on locked doors.
Screams for help go unheard.
Bitter tears stream from bloodshot eyes,
keeping us locked in the closets of our lives

The turn of a key is faintly heard.
The call of a voice softly through the door
brings signs of faint rays of light
as someone opens the closets of our lives.

A day of hope has arrived.
Help comes at long, long last
as a smiling face is seen in the bright of the day
freeing us from the closets of our lives.

*Dedicated to all of those individuals who feel trapped
in the darkness of their lives and to all of those persons
who aid in unlocking the closets of their lives.*

The Window

Protected from life,
hidden from view,
alone in my room
With little to do.
I sit at my window,
safe from the world,
looking out at people
going about in a swirl.

Whether a marriage or loved one
who has been lost
or maybe a business of which I was once boss,
now all is gone and with nothing to do,
I sit at my window,
safe from the world
and hidden from view.

A world of hurt
do I see.
A retreat from life
is safer for me.

Like an animal hurt and
withdrawing from life,
hiding from the world and all of its strife,
I sit at my window
with nothing to do,
not willing to commit to the care of a few.

There was a time
in this life I know
when I would come and I would go.
Now I hide away from it all,
not willing to venture out from this closed-in stall.

With nothing but a window
to the world that I see,
hidden from sight
and all who would love me.
A sad time is had.
A lost life is bad.
But my window is all that I allow to protect me.

The Slave

From a faraway land, he was brought in chains.
In a dark hole of a black ship, he was sold for gains.
His life belonged to another,
and to the highest bidder he was sold to his keeper's brother.
He worked from first light to past the setting sun.
And then did more until the work was done.
Six days a week, with rest on one,
he toiled at hard labor under the scorch of the sun.
The crack of a whip
brought no words from his lips.
He just looked down
and worked without a sound.
For his labors he received not a cent.
He did and went where he was sent.
A crude shelter he called his home.
Worn clothes were all that covered his bones.
Of family he was not allowed any.
And friends, truly, there were not very many.
When his life was ended, in a rude bed he was laid
and his worn body then placed in an unmarked grave.

Fading Memory

✦

Things can come and things can go
with a mind that has become so slow.
I cannot keep a thought for long
as I continue to go along.

This river of time I find myself in
just keeps on going and I can't remember when.
My thoughts stay jumbled and finally lost.
Will I not be able to have a mind on the mend?

Age and memory aren't much fun
when that river of time keeps going and you have none.
A fading mind is like a day that is ending.
All that's left is a thought that needs mending.

Misty Rain

Misty rain is all I see.
Misty rain all around me.
Lost in the storms of life somewhere.
It's almost more than a soul can bear.

Time is an ever-rolling thing,
losing friends in a never-ending game.
Lost forever in a world not the same,
darken skies shedding its rain.

A veil of time like a sentinel stands,
waiting for the summons to enter its land.
Many a friend is lost to its call.
All will enter this misty wall.

Misty rain is all I see.
Misty rain all around me.
Tell this story to all around.
Friends depart and are not to be found.

Walk in a world dark and gray
without old friends to light the way.
Misty rain is all I see.
Misty rain all around me.

When in time a summons I hear,
to my earthly cradle I go without fear.
There my old friends, with arms open wide,
will lead me to the other side.

From that misty veil one cannot hide.
All must enter to get to the other side.
A time of joy follows a day of tears,
As friends are waiting to remove all our fears.

Section IV
SUMMONS OF TIME

On the Wings of an Eagle

If I had the wings of an eagle,
I would soar to the heights of the sky
to look down on the beauty of life itself
and the marvels of creation from on high.

I can imagine all that our Creator does see
as He watches from heaven above,
every creature, every thing that He has made,
every beauty, each thing how He must love.

If I had the wings of an eagle,
I would soar to the heights of the sky
to look down on the beauty of life itself
and the marvels of creation from on high.

Can you imagine what it would feel like
to soar through the clouds way up above,
to kiss the edge of heaven itself
and feel the touch of God's own love?

Oh, if I had the wings of an eagle,
how I could feel so free from earth beneath.
To soar to the very heights of the sky,
and enjoy the quiet of the clouds soaring by.

If I had the wings of an eagle,
I would soar to the heights of the sky
to look down on the beauty of life itself
and the marvels of creation from on high.

Heaven's Gate

There is a place far from here,
yet not so far, but really near.
A place whose door is open wide,
a place where everyone is welcomed inside.
Heaven's Gate is its name.
It's a place where all who enter are treated the same.
It is the door to a place of rest,
for all who enter are treated with the best.
A place where calm and peace prevail,
where beauty and love are not for sale.
All are given free and clear,
a home for all with nothing but cheer.
It was bought with the life of the One inside,
given to us as a sign of His love,
and marked on the door is a descending dove.
It is a place where there is no envy or hate,
and all who come are welcome to enter Heaven's Gate.

My Right Hand

My right hand is my strength and my guide.
He is always by my side.

My right hand is my leader and friend.
It is to him I turn when my life is in need of a mend.

My right hand is the one I lean on the most.
He is the one who guides me when I feel lost.

My right hand is the one who shows me the way,
the one to whom I speak to first before I have my say.

He is the one whom I trust
whenever I have gotten into a fuss.

When fear tries to take control of my life,
I turn to my right hand to lead me from the strife.

When I feel lost and don't know what to do,
my right hand is always present and leads me out of my stew.

I would give my life for my right hand to stay free,
just as He has already done for me.

Adapted from Psalm 16:8

There Is a River Deep and Wide

❧✦❦

There is a river deep and wide.
I am bound to find a way to the other side.
I have labored here long and hard,
and now I long just to see my Lord.

There is a time for everything in life, we are told,
work and play and friends and all I've had.
But all I have done is work to the bone.
Now I just want to go on home.

There is a river deep and wide.
I am bound to find a way to the other side.
I have labored here long and hard
and now I long just to see my Lord.

Many a friend, foe, and kin have all left this land
and now have taken their stand
on the banks of that river deep and wide.
Now I am left to stand alone,
looking for a way to the other side.

There is a river deep and wide.
I am bound to find a way to the other side.
I have labored here long and hard
and now I long just to see my Lord.

There is a glorious day coming
when I cross that river deep and wide
To take my stand on the other side.
For I have labored here long and hard,
and then I will be with my beloved Lord.

This was written following the funeral of a good friend who
passed away following a very long battle with cancer.

There Is a Grace in This Land

There is a grace in this land
that comes from One who is close at hand,
not from that which I can do,
but a gift from the One whose voice is my command.

I walk through life as though a ghost,
not knowing from one day to the next
just what I am to do,
but guided by One who knows that I am perplexed.

Faith and trust is the command.
I wait in hope of serving the Man.
And then a voice do I hear,
"Go and tell them who I am."

Time and again, I asked for His word
to let me hear in my time of fear.
In the dark, I cried out, "Lord, I hurt."
Then I heard, "I'm here!"

There is a grace in this land
that comes from One who is close at hand,
not from that which I can do,
but a gift from One whose voice is my command.

Times of trouble and hurt I have seen.
By my efforts, nothing could make me clean.
It was the grace from Him above
that saved this wretch with nothing but His love.

There is a grace in this land
that comes from one who is close at hand,
not from that which I can do,
but from a gift from One whose voice is my command.

I Heard a Voice in Nighttime Calling

I heard a voice in the nighttime calling,
as soft and gentle as a summer breeze.
I heard a voice in the nighttime calling.
It flowed about me as a gentle wind through the trees.

I heard a voice in the nighttime calling,
one that was as clear as a lark in the trees,
a sound that made me wonder
if the call was coming on a far-off breeze.

My heart leapt at the sound,
so gentle and yet so real.
It made me wonder if I were dreaming.
It all seemed just so surreal.

I heard a voice in the nighttime calling,
as soft and gentle as a summer breeze.
I rose in the night, looked far and near,
and answering, said, *I am here.*

When a voice is heard in the nighttime calling,
as soft and gentle as a summer breeze,
when a voice is heard in the nighttime calling
that it seems to flow as a gentle wind through the trees,
it is a voice calling each of us,
a voice from far, yet so near.
It is the voice of the blessed One
seeking one to come here.

Jesus

He came to us in the night,
born in a stable, long ago,
with only the stars for light,
a sign of heaven's glow.
Wrapped in a blanket
and warmed by love,
He became a sign
of God's descending dove.

He came to teach
of a new word of God,
one of mercy and of love
and with a promise from above.
He healed the sick,
cured the lame,
gave sight to the blind,
and raised the dead.
He was the Son of God,
the one true Lamb,
sent to us all
from that night in a stall.

Jesus was his name,
Immanuel — God with us,
the Prince of Peace.
But a jealous and frightened few
incited the people into a stew
and beat and tormented Him
and nailed Him to a tree.
So He died without any blame
that we might be free of our shame.
But God raised Him from the dead
and overcame all strife,
that we in turn might have eternal life.

About the Author: Big

Known as Big Daddy to the kids—shortened just to Big—Richard G. Moriarty worked every day for the past fifty years in finance, personnel, and retirement system management. He has been the recipient of Who's Who in Government and Who's Who in Finance and Industry. Moriarty was twice the recipient of the Charles Dunbar Career Public Service Award. He has been senior warden of his Episcopal church, as well as a lector and lay reader. He has been a Kiwanis Club past vice-president and secretary-treasurer and a Rotary Club past-president and treasurer. He was a recipient of the Service Above Self Award from Rotary International. He has been a Paul Harris Fellow of Rotary International. He has been named United Way Division Chairman.

Work by Moriarty includes an autobiography, *My Early Years: Richard Graham Moriarty,* and *A History: 150 years of Service: Trinity Episcopal Church, Cheneyville, Louisiana.* In addition, he created and narrated a DVD on the same subject. He has also written a short history, *The Wells Brothers of Rapides Parish, Breeders of Champion Horses.* Moriarty is currently working on a new novel, *Wilderness Man.*

The author wishes to express a word of personal appreciation to Diana Bogardus for the illustrations so beautifully done and all her efforts in assisting the author with the layout of *Rivers of Time*

CPSIA information can be obtained at www.ICGtesting.com
Printed in the USA
LVOW120948220912

299821LV00002B/1/P